HAL•LEONARD®

GUITAR PLAY-ALONG

AUDIO ACCESS INCLUDED

PLAYBACK+
Speed · Pitch · Balance · Loop

VOL. 5

THREE CHORD
SONGS

T0070949

To access audio visit:
www.halleonard.com/mylibrary

Enter Code
2955-4663-8993-5936

ISBN 978-1-5400-6354-0

HAL•LEONARD®

Visit Hal Leonard Online at
www.halleonard.com

Contact us:
Hal Leonard
7777 West Bluemound Road
Milwaukee, WI 53213
Email: info@halleonard.com

In Europe, contact:
Hal Leonard Europe Limited
42 Wigmore Street
Marylebone, London, W1U 2RN
Email: info@halleonardeurope.com

In Australia, contact:
Hal Leonard Australia Pty. Ltd.
4 Lentara Court
Cheltenham, Victoria, 3192 Australia
Email: info@halleonard.com.au

Guitar Notation Legend

THE MUSICAL STAFF shows pitches and rhythms and is divided by bar lines into measures. Pitches are named after the first seven letters of the alphabet.

TABLATURE graphically represents the guitar fingerboard. Each horizontal line represents a string, and each number represents a fret.

4th string, 2nd fret   1st & 2nd strings open, played together   open D chord

HALF-STEP BEND: Strike the note and bend up 1/2 step.

WHOLE-STEP BEND: Strike the note and bend up one step.

GRACE NOTE BEND: Strike the note and immediately bend up as indicated.

SLIGHT (MICROTONE) BEND: Strike the note and bend up 1/4 step.

BEND AND RELEASE: Strike the note and bend up as indicated, then release back to the original note. Only the first note is struck.

PRE-BEND: Bend the note as indicated, then strike it.

VIBRATO: The string is vibrated by rapidly bending and releasing the note with the fretting hand.

PALM MUTING: The note is partially muted by the pick hand lightly touching the string(s) just before the bridge.

HAMMER-ON: Strike the first (lower) note with one finger, then sound the higher note (on the same string) with another finger by fretting it without picking.

PULL-OFF: Place both fingers on the notes to be sounded. Strike the first note and without picking, pull the finger off to sound the second (lower) note.

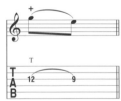

LEGATO SLIDE: Strike the first note and then slide the same fret-hand finger up or down to the second note. The second note is not struck.

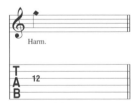

SHIFT SLIDE: Same as legato slide, except the second note is struck.

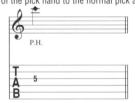

TRILL: Very rapidly alternate between the notes indicated by continuously hammering on and pulling off.

TAPPING: Hammer ("tap") the fret indicated with the pick-hand index or middle finger and pull off to the note fretted by the fret hand.

NATURAL HARMONIC: Strike the note while the fret-hand lightly touches the string directly over the fret indicated.

PINCH HARMONIC: The note is fretted normally and a harmonic is produced by adding the edge of the thumb or the tip of the index finger of the pick hand to the normal pick attack.

TREMOLO PICKING: The note is picked as rapidly and continuously as possible.

VIBRATO BAR DIVE AND RETURN: The pitch of the note or chord is dropped a specified number of steps (in rhythm), then returned to the original pitch.

VIBRATO BAR SCOOP: Depress the bar just before striking the note, then quickly release the bar.

VIBRATO BAR DIP: Strike the note and then immediately drop a specified number of steps, then release back to the original pitch.

Additional Musical Definitions

(accent)   • Accentuate note (play it louder).

(staccato)   • Play the note short.

D.S. al Coda   • Go back to the sign (𝄋), then play until the measure marked "*To Coda*," then skip to the section labelled "**Coda**."

D.C. al Fine   • Go back to the beginning of the song and play until the measure marked "***Fine***" (end).

Fill

N.C.

• Label used to identify a brief melodic figure which is to be inserted into the arrangement.

• Harmony is implied.

• Repeat measures between signs.

• When a repeated section has different endings, play the first ending only the first time and the second ending only the second time.

CONTENTS

Breakdown

Words and Music by Tom Petty

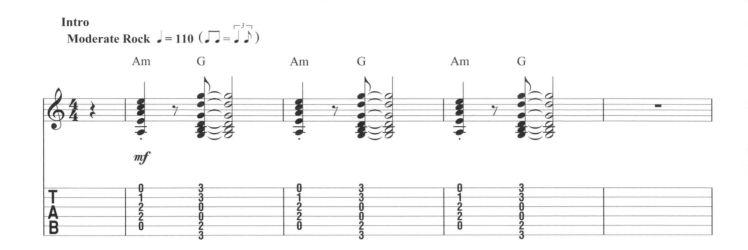

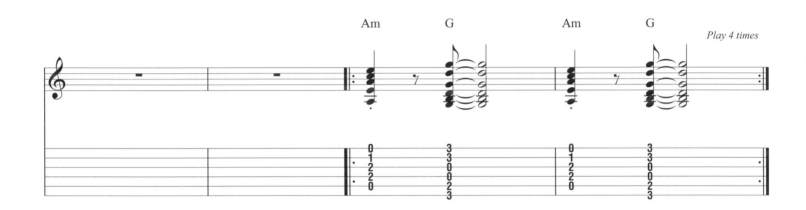

1. It's al-right if you love me; it's al-right if you
2. *See additional lyrics*

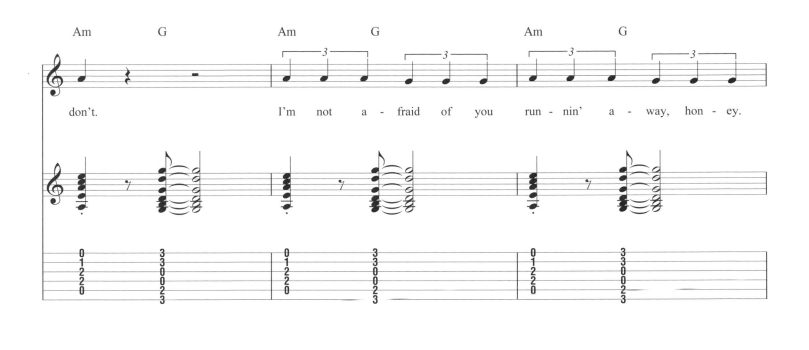

don't.　　I'm not a-fraid of you run-nin' a-way, hon-ey.

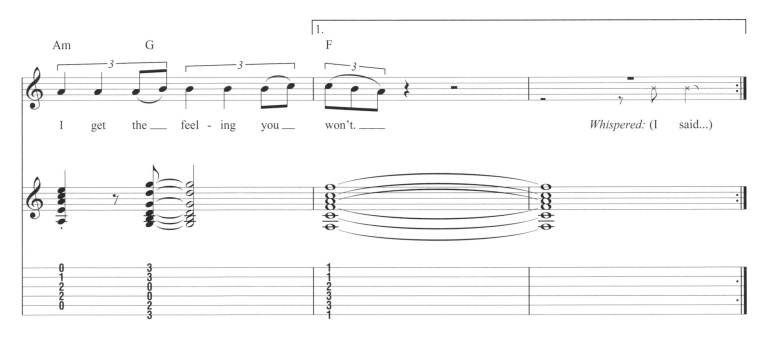

I get the ___ feel-ing you ___ won't. ___　*Whispered:* (I said...)

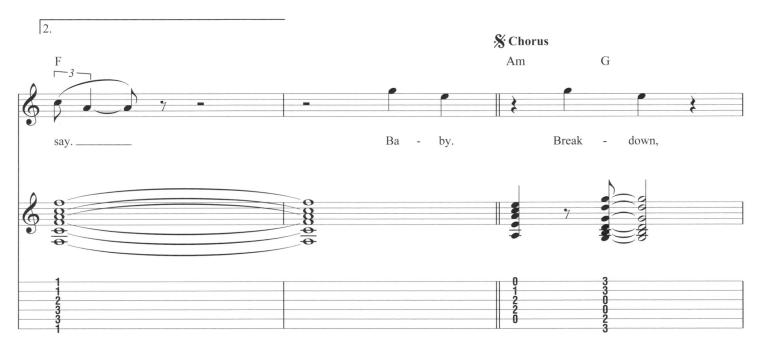

say. _____　　　Ba - by.　　Break - down,

%Chorus

5

go a-head, give it to me. Break - down, hon-ey, take ___ me through the night.

Break - down, now I'm stand - in' here, can you see? Break - down, it's al -

To Coda ⊕

right. ___ It's al - right. ___ It's al -

Interlude

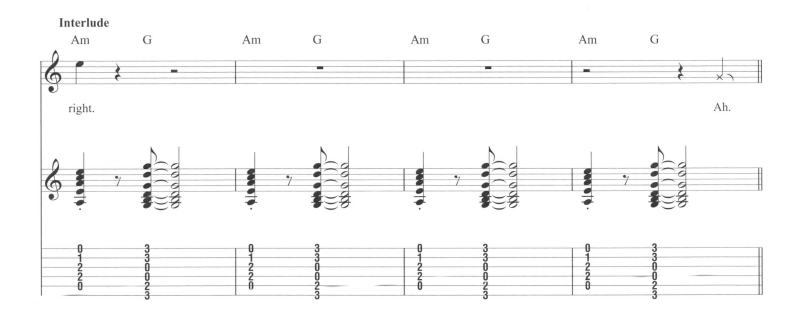

right.   Ah.

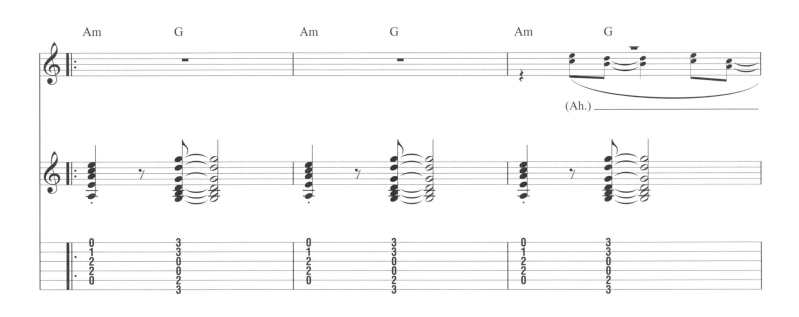

(Ah.) ——————————————

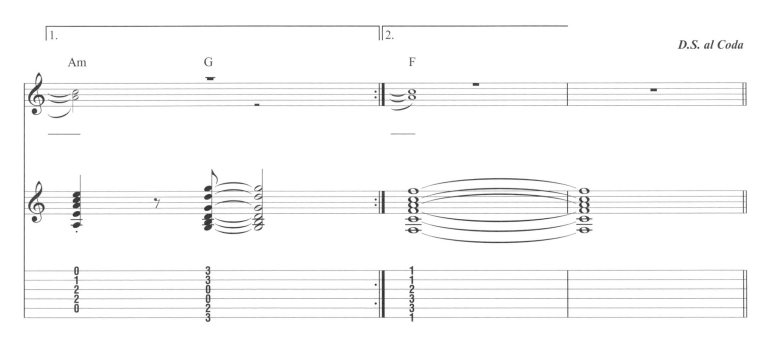

D.S. al Coda

Coda

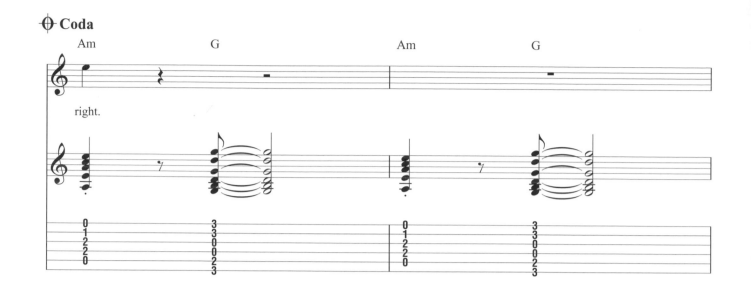

right.

Outro

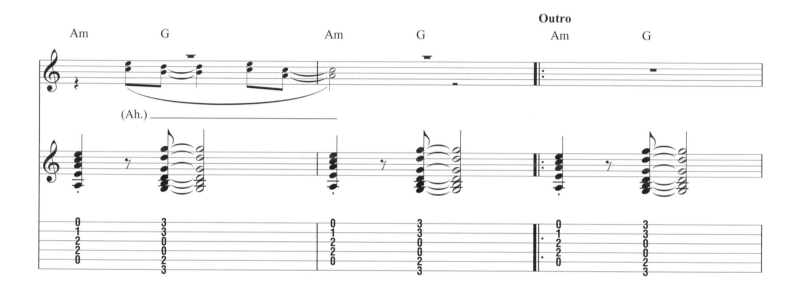

(Ah.)

Repeat and fade

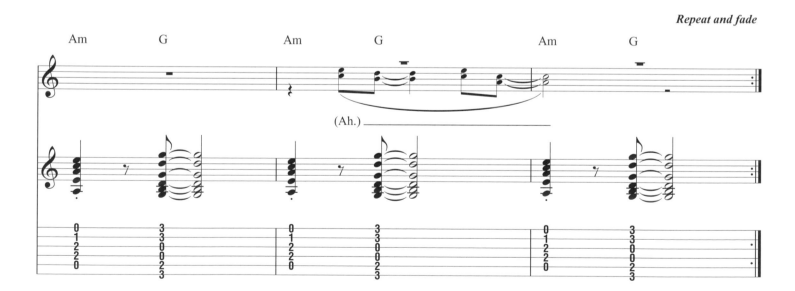

(Ah.)

Additional Lyrics

2. There is no sense in pretending;
   Your eyes give you away.
   Somethin' inside you is feelin' like I do.
   We've said all there is to say.

Ring of Fire

Words and Music by Merle Kilgore and June Carter

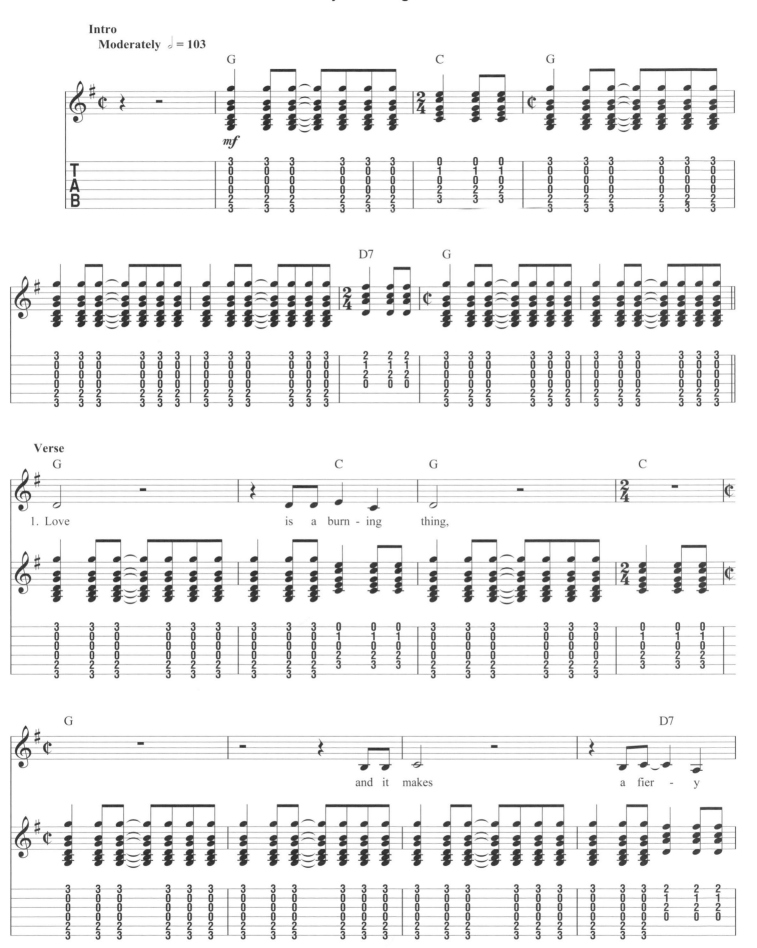

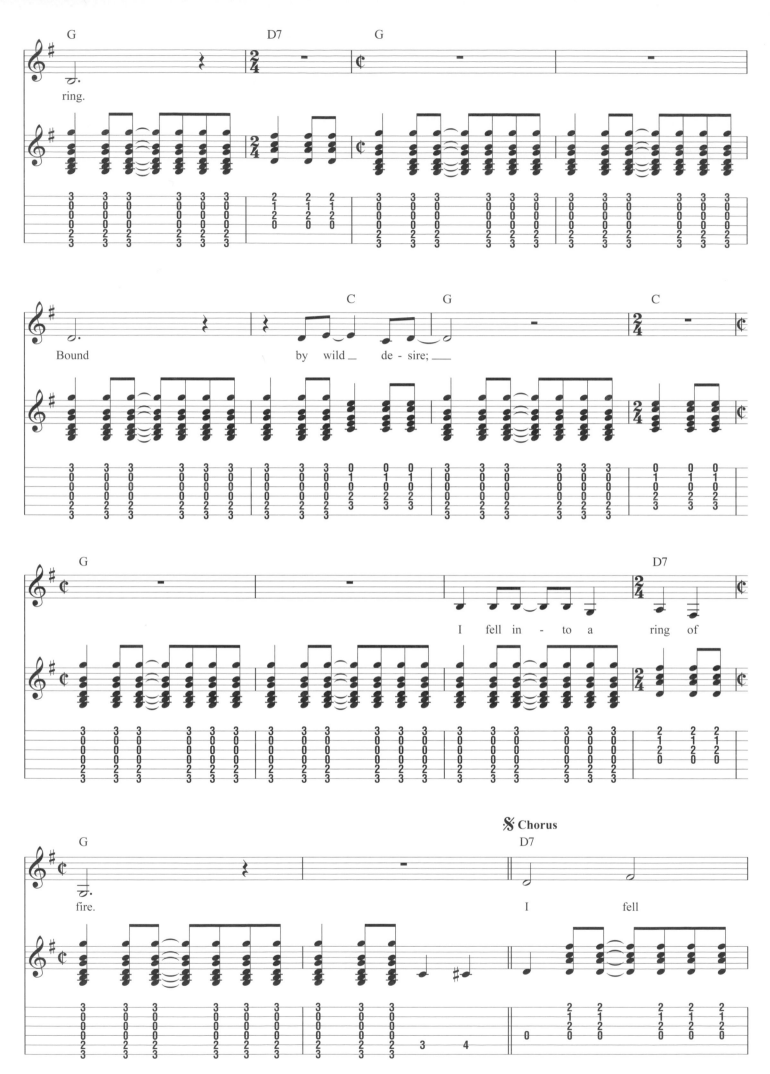

§ Chorus

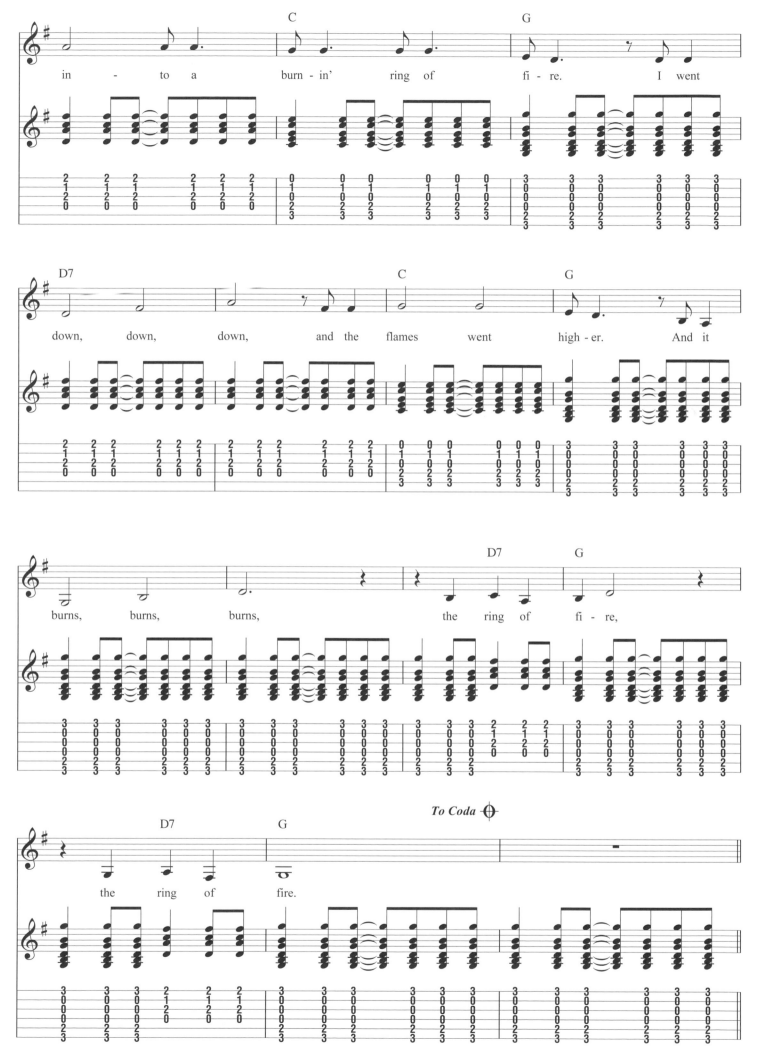

Interlude

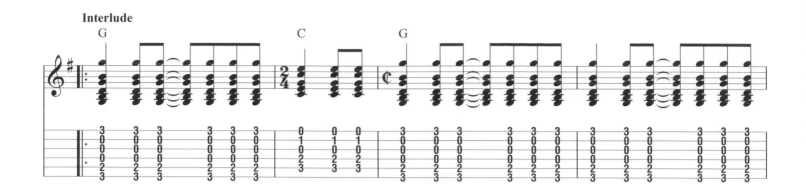

2nd time, D.S. al Coda

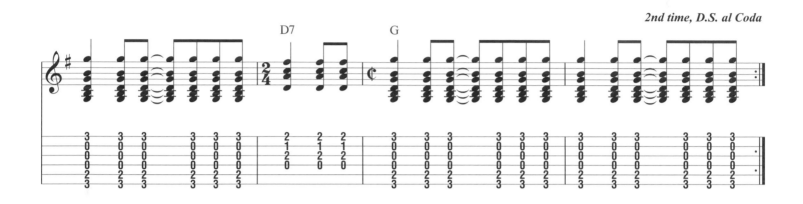

Coda

Verse

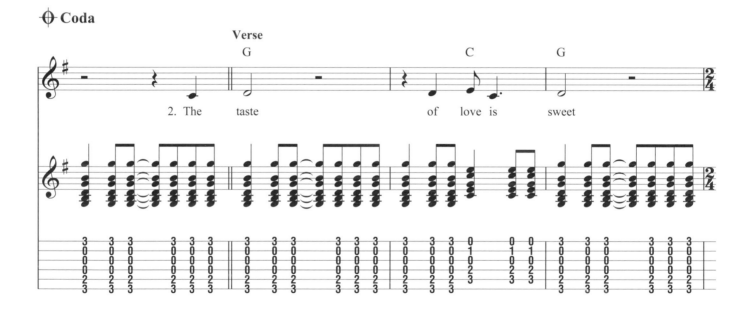

2. The taste of love is sweet

when hearts

like ours ___ meet.

I fell for you like a child. ___

Oh, ___ but the fire went wild. ___

Chorus

Love Me Do

Words and Music by John Lennon and Paul McCartney

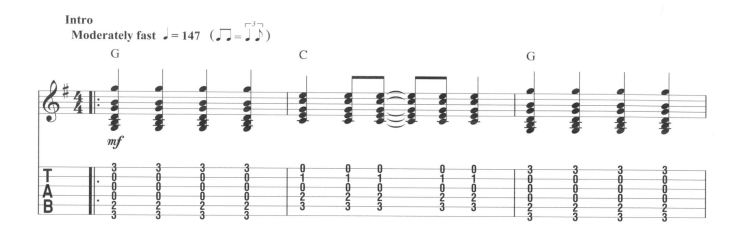

1. - 4. Love,   love me do, _____   you

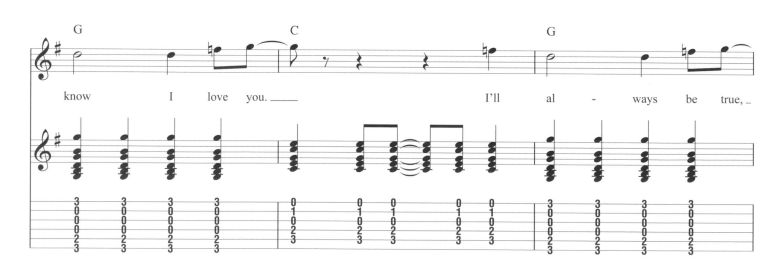

know   I love you. _____   I'll al - ways be true,_

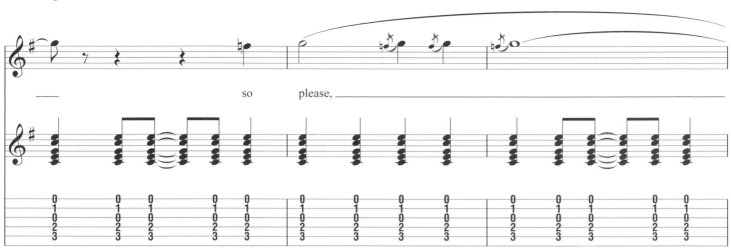

so please, _____

Chorus
To Coda 2 ⊕

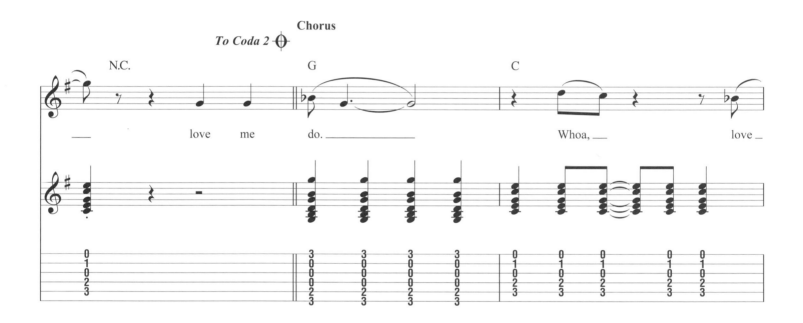

love me do. _____ Whoa, _____ love _____

To Coda 1 ⊕

|1. |2. **Bridge**

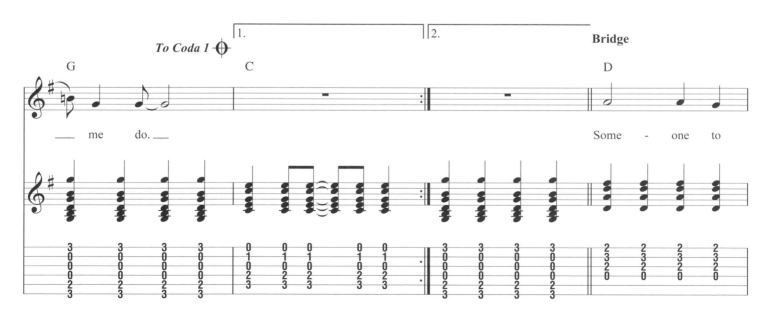

_____ me do. _____ Some - one to

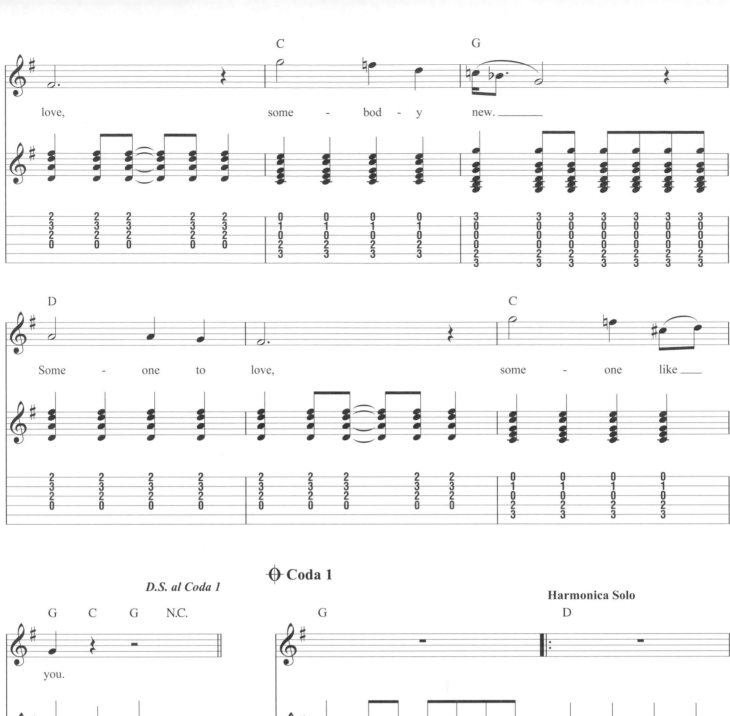

love, some-bod-y new. _____

Some - one to love, some - one like _____

⊕ Coda 1

D.S. al Coda 1

you.

Harmonica Solo

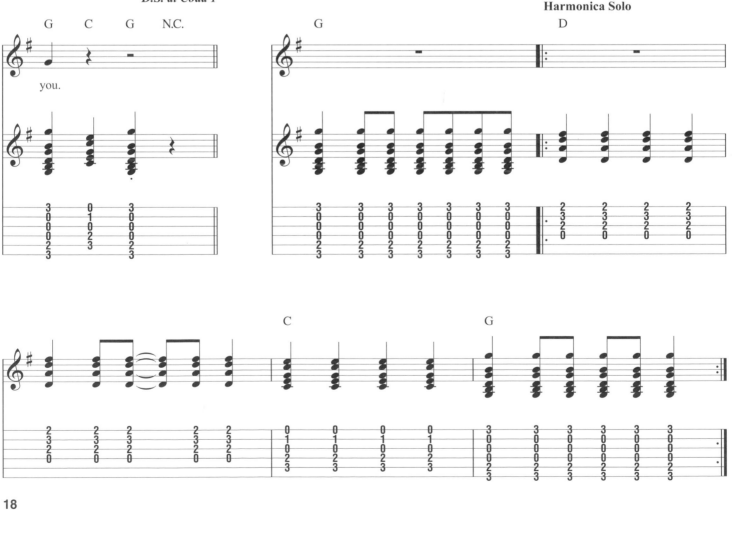

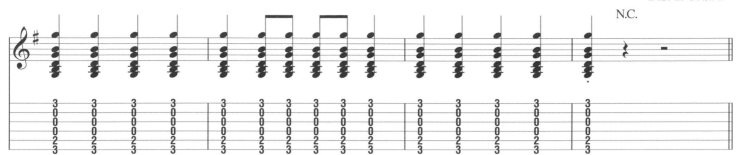

N.C.

Coda 2

Chorus

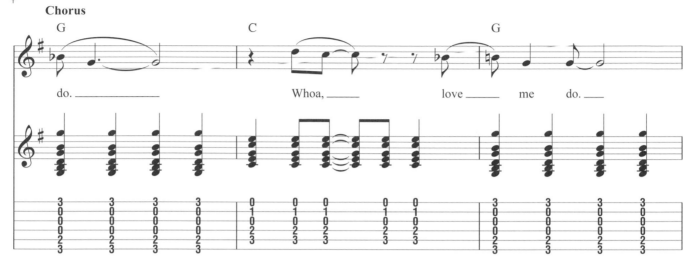

do. _____ Whoa, _____ love _____ me do. _____

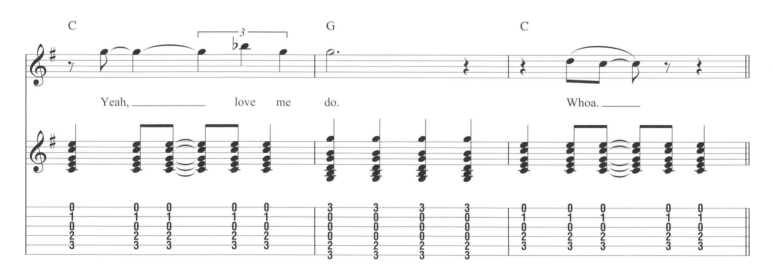

Yeah, _____ love me do. Whoa. _____

Outro

Repeat and fade

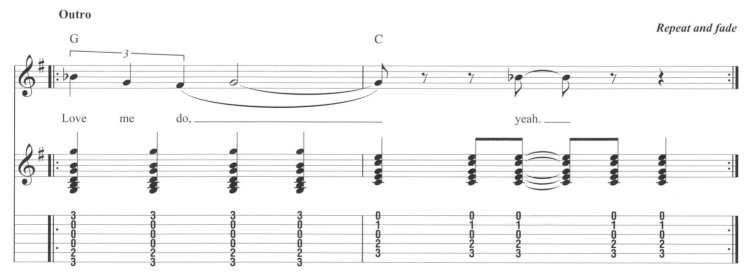

Love me do, yeah. _____

Margaritaville

Words and Music by Jimmy Buffett

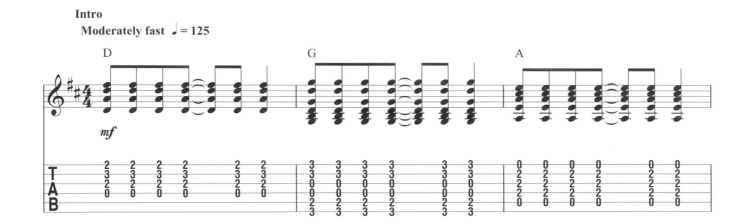

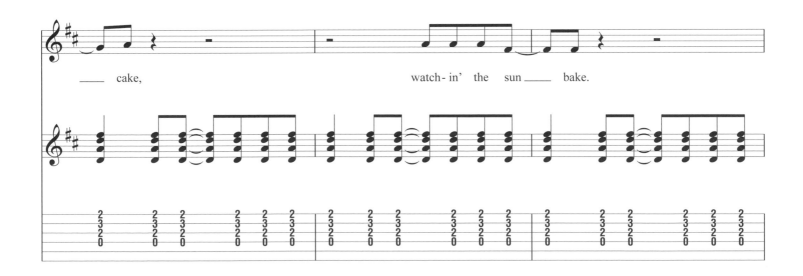

all of those tour - ists cov - ered with oil. _____

Strum - min' my six - string

on _____ my front porch _____ swing. Smell those shrimp, _____

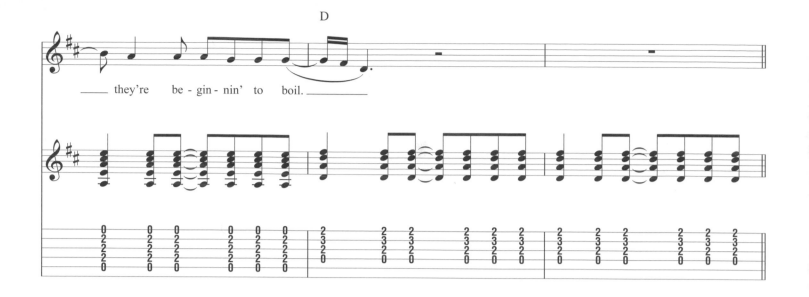

they're be - gin - nin' to boil.

Chorus

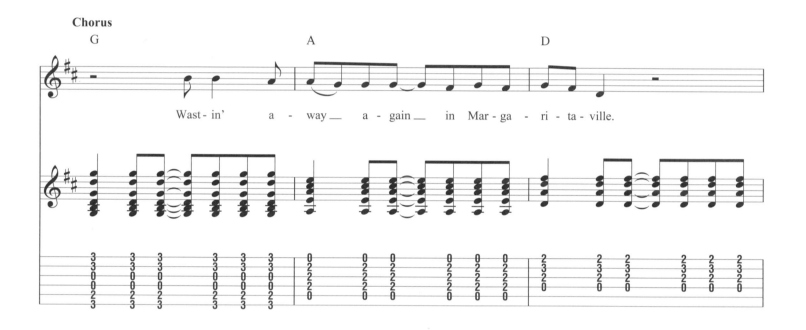

Wast - in' a - way __ a - gain __ in Mar - ga - ri - ta - ville.

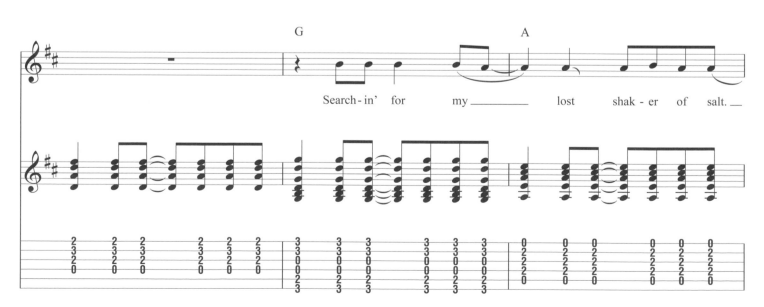

Search - in' for my _____ lost shak - er of salt. __

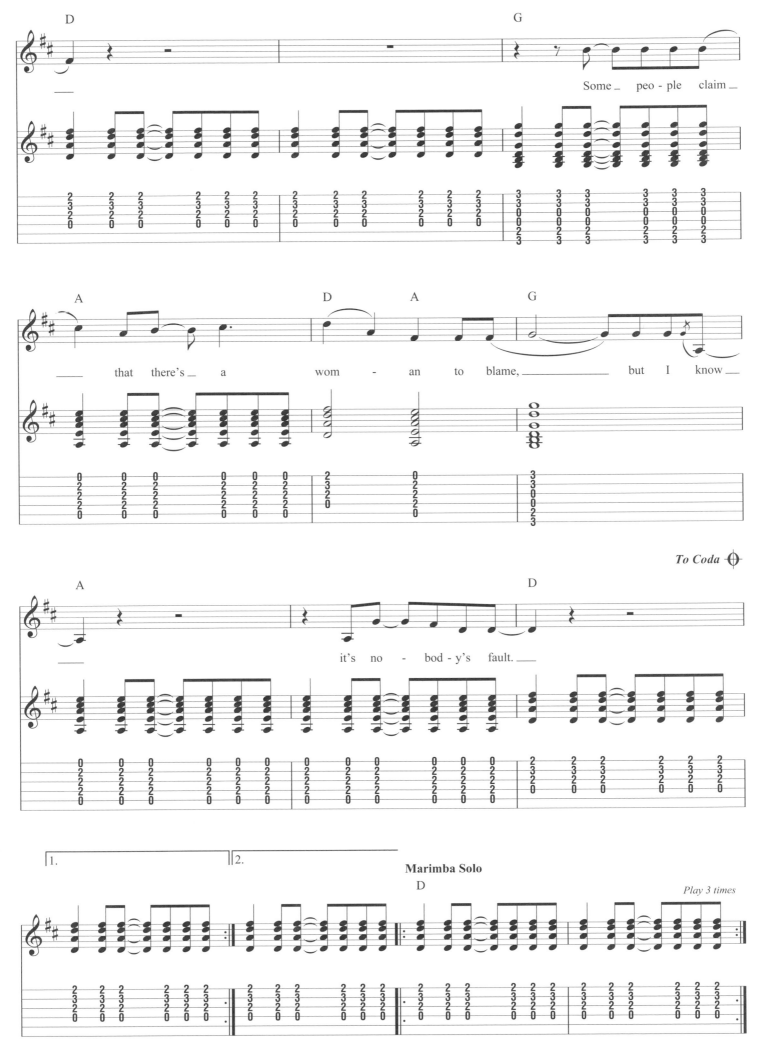

To Coda ⊕

Marimba Solo

Play 3 times

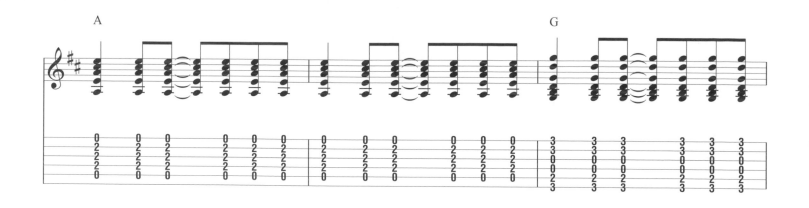

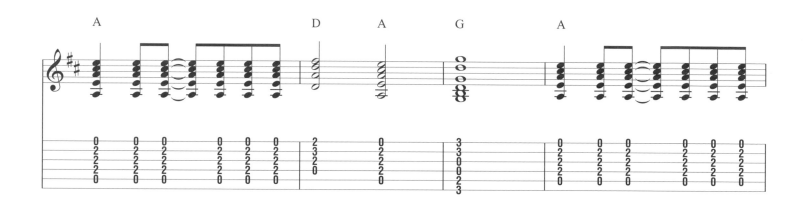

D.S. al Coda

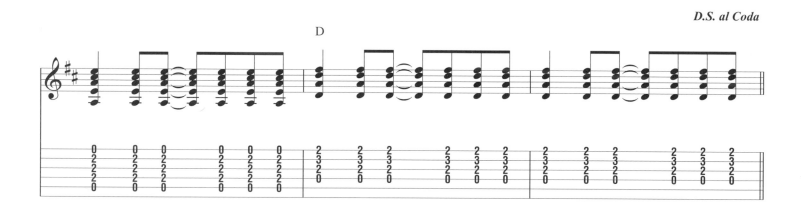

$\oplus$ **Coda**

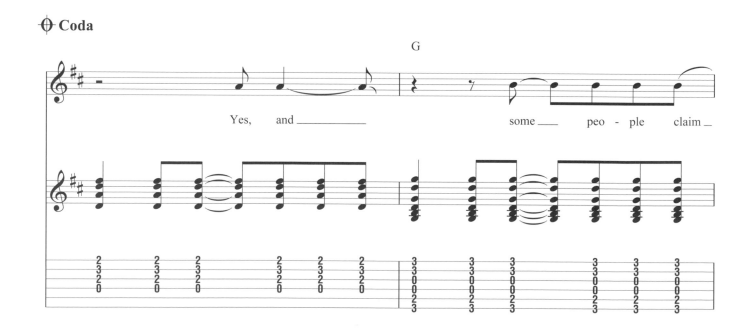

Yes,   and _____   some ___ peo - ple claim __

24

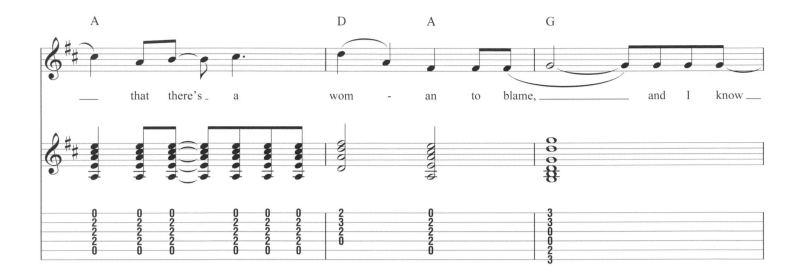

that there's a wom-an to blame, _____ and I know __

Outro

__ it's my own __ damn __ fault. __

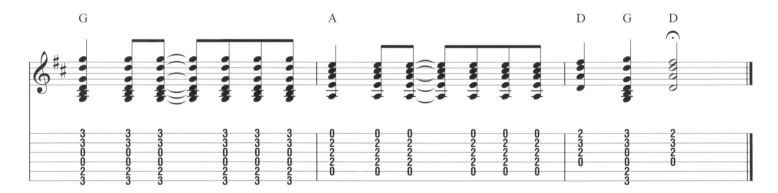

Additional Lyrics

2. Don't know the reason
   I stayed here all season.
   Nothin' to show but this brand-new tattoo.
   But it's a real beauty,
   A Mexican cutie.
   How it got here, I haven't a clue.

3. I blew out my flip-flop;
   Stepped on a pop-top.
   Cut my heal, had to cruise on back home.
   But there's booze in the blender,
   And soon it will render
   That frozen concoction that helps me hang on.

Rock and Roll Music

Words and Music by Chuck Berry

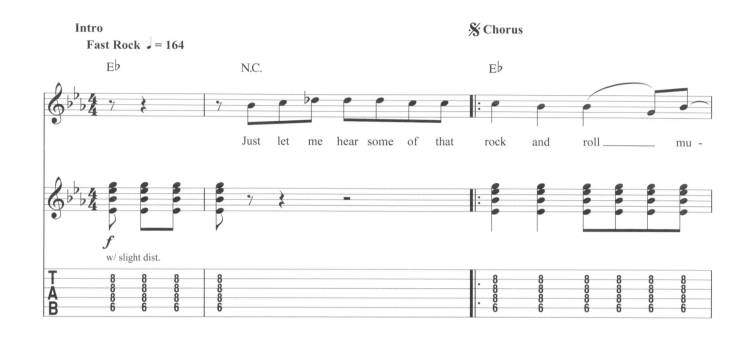

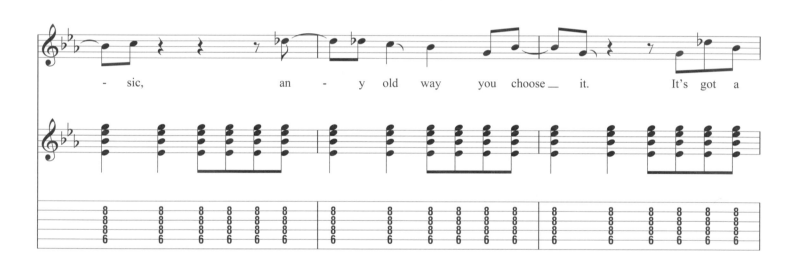

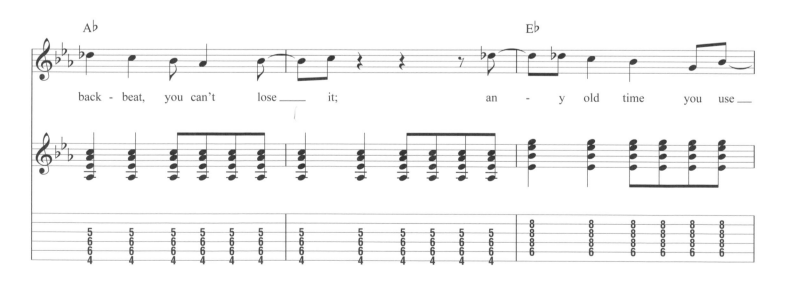

It's got-ta be rock 'n' roll mu - sic if

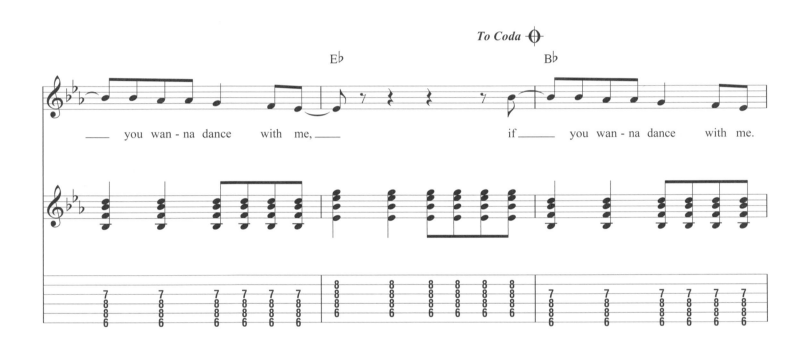

you wan - na dance with me, if you wan - na dance with me.

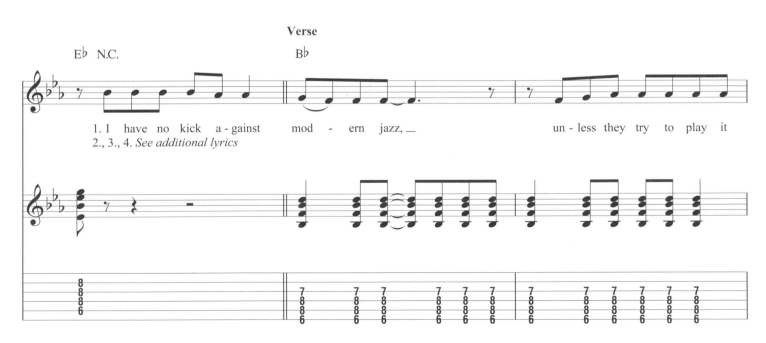

1. I have no kick a - gainst mod - ern jazz, un - less they try to play it
2., 3., 4. *See additional lyrics*

4th time, D.S. al Coda

Additional Lyrics

2. I took my loved one over 'cross the tracks
   So she could hear my man a-wailin' sax.
   I must admit they have a rockin' band.
   Man, they were blowin' like a hurrican'.
   That's why I go for that...

3. Way down South they gave a jubilee,
   Them country folks, they had a jamboree.
   They're drinkin' home brew from a wooden cup;
   The folks dancin' got all shook up.
   And started playin' that...

4. Don't care to hear 'em play a tango;
   I'm in no mood to dig a mambo.
   It's way too early for the congo,
   So keep a-rockin' that piano.
   So I can hear some of that...

Stir It Up

Words and Music by Bob Marley

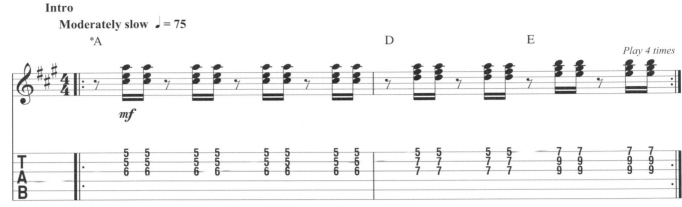

*Touch strings at indicated fret locations but don't push down to the fretboard.

now   you   are   here. __   I __ say   it's   o - kay __   to

see   what - a   we   will   do,   ba - by,   just __ me   and __ you.   Come on and

Chorus

stir   it   up, __   I   wan - na   say,   lit - tle   dar - lin', yeah.

Stir   it   up, __   come on, ba - by.   Come on and

Stir it up, ___ yeah, ___ lit - tle dar - lin'.

Stir it up, ___ oh, ___ mm. 2. It's

Verse

time to push the wood, and I'll blaze your ___ fire. ___

Then I sat - is - fy ___ your all de - sire, ___

Outro-Chorus

Repeat and fade

Walk of Life

Words and Music by Mark Knopfler

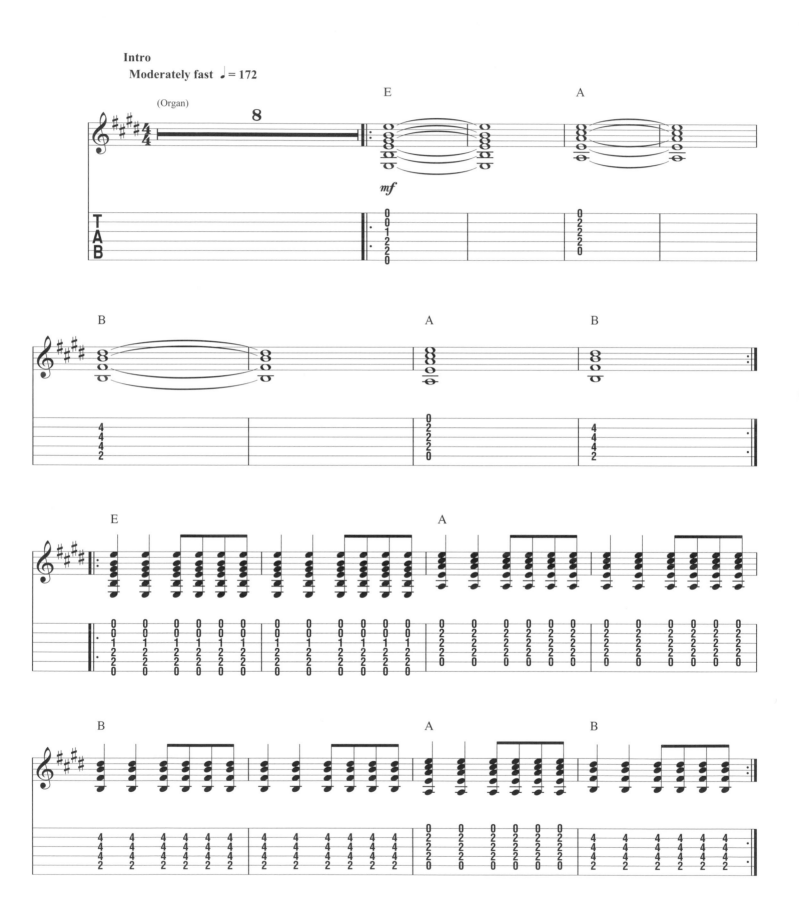

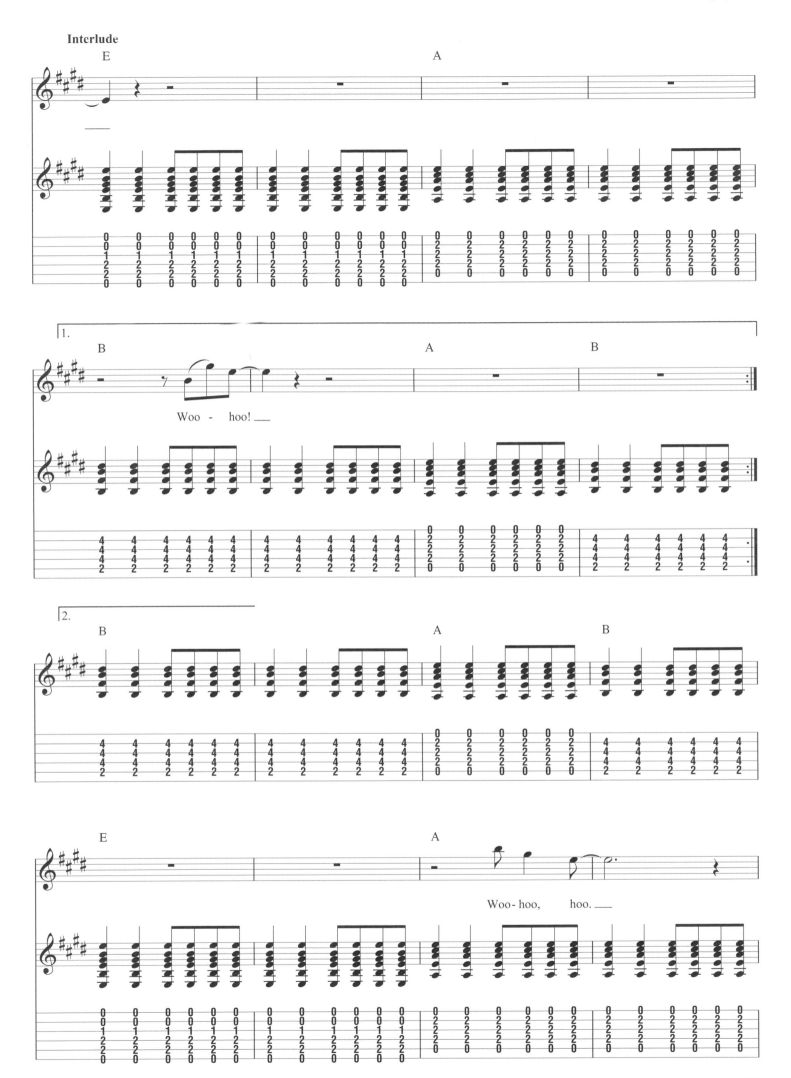

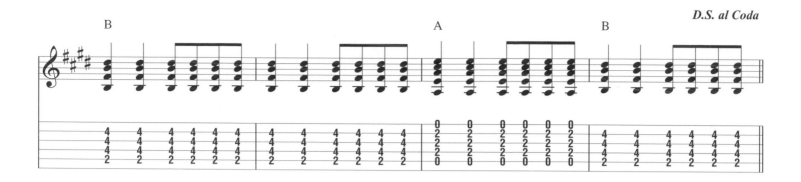

⊕ Coda

in-to the day. __ And af-ter all the vi-o-lence and dou-ble-talk, there's just a

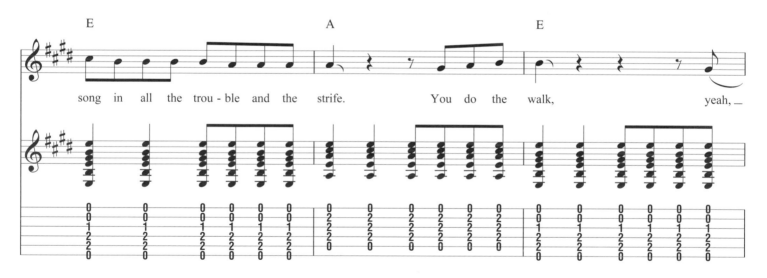

song in all the trou-ble and the strife. You do the walk, yeah, __

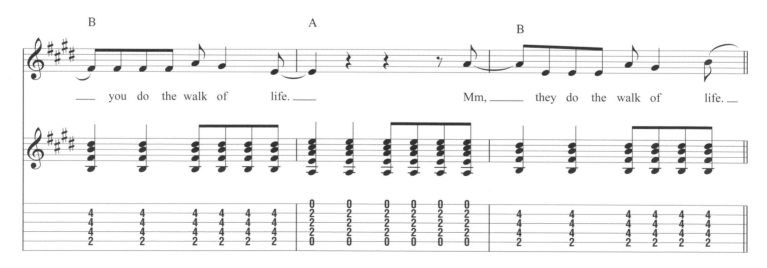

__ you do the walk of life. ___ Mm, ___ they do the walk of life. __

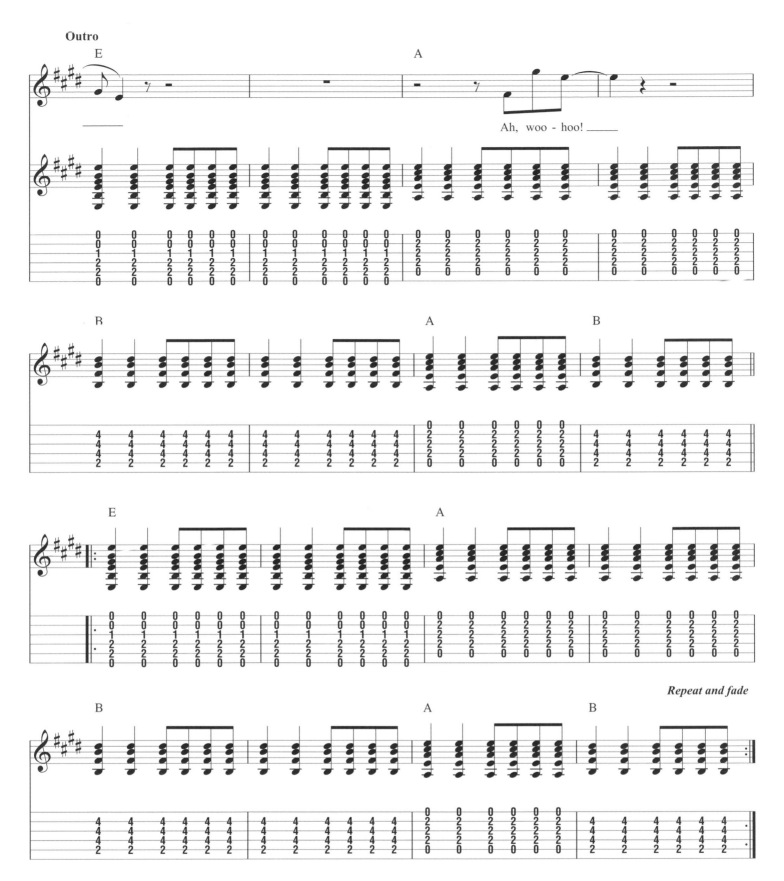

Additional Lyrics

2. Here come Johnny, gonna tell you the story.
   Hand me down my walkin' shoes.
   Here come Johnny with the power and the glory.
   Backbeat, the talkin' blues.
   He got the action, he got the motion.
   Man, the boy can play.
   Dedication, devotion.
   Turning all the nighttime into the day.
   Do the song about the sweet, lovin' woman,
   They do the song about the knife.
   Man, they do the walk, do the walk of life.
   Yeah, you do the walk of life.

You Don't Mess Around with Jim

Words and Music by Jim Croce

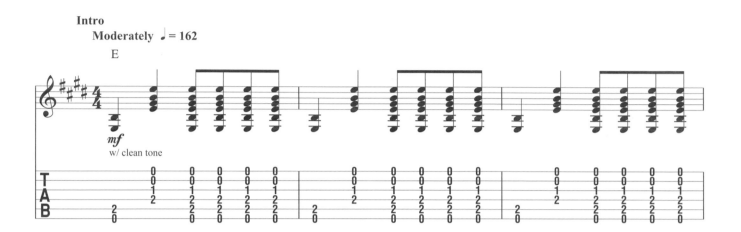

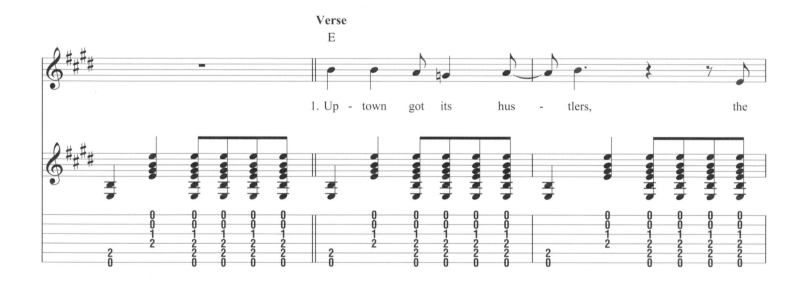

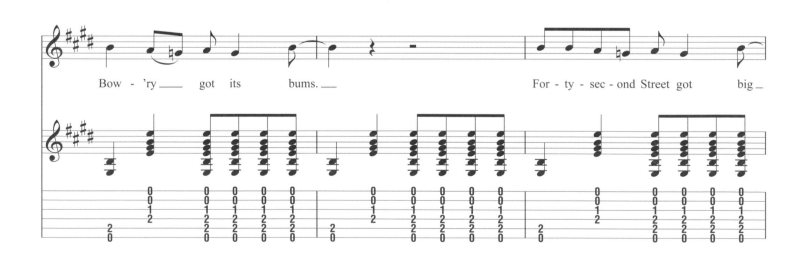

Jim a Walk - er, he a pool shoot - in' son of a gun. ___ Yeah, he big ___

and ___ dumb ___ as a man ___ can come ___ but he strong - er than a coun - try hoss. ___

And when the bad folks all get to - geth - er at night, ___ you know they

all call ___ big Jim ___ "Boss" ___ just ___ be - cause. ___

Chorus

And they say, __ "You don't tug on Su - per-man's cape. You don't spit in - to the wind. __ You don't pull the mask off the old Lone Rang - er and you don't mess a - round with __ Jim." __ A doo, doo, da, da, dee, dee, dee, dee, dee, dee. 2. Well, out - ta

44

Verse

South Al-a-bam-a come a coun-try boy. He said, "I'm look-in' for a man named Jim, ___

3. See additional lyrics

___ I am a pool shoot-in' boy, my name is Wil-lie Mc-Coy ___ but down

home they call me Slim. ___ Yeah, I'm look - in' for the King of For-ty-

sec - ond Street, he driv-in' a drop - top Cad-il-lac. Last week he took ___

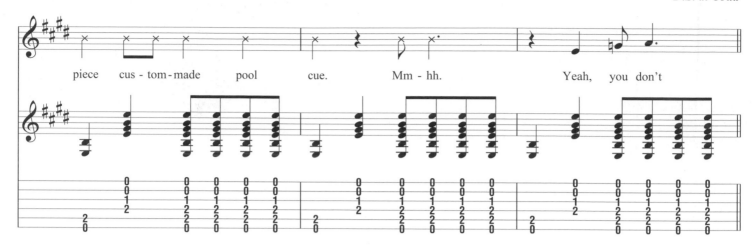

piece cus-tom-made pool cue. Mm - hh. Yeah, you don't

Coda

Outro

E

Mm, mm, mm, mm, mm, mm, mm, mm. Mm, mm, mm, mm.

Repeat and fade

Mm, mm, mm, mm, mm, mm, mm, mm. Mm, mm, mm, mm.

Additional Lyrics

3. Well, a hush fell over the poolroom,
   Jimmy come boppin' in off the street.
   And when the cuttin' were done,
   The only part that wasn't bloody was
   The soles of the big man's feet. Woo!
   Yeah, he were cut in 'bout a hundred places,
   And he were shot in a couple more.
   And you better believe they sung a diff'rent kind of story
   When a big Jim hit the floor.
   Oh. Now they say you don't...